Mission to Millions

How to find your Passion and Purpose in life

MAKING MONEY WITH YOUR PASSION

LUCHO

Mission to Millions:

How to find your Passion and Purpose in life

Mission to Millions:

How to find your Passion and Purpose in life

For my mama

Mission to Millions:

How to find your Passion and Purpose in life

Mission to Millions:
How to find your Passion and Purpose in life

"Purpose is the reason you journey. Passion is the fire that lights your way."

-Anonymous

Mission to Millions:

How to find your Passion and Purpose in life

Introduction

I want to thank you and congratulate you for downloading the book, *"Mission to Millions: How to Find Your Passion and Purpose in life"*.

This book has powerful information that will help you to discover your personal mission and create a successful vision.

We all want one thing in life: massive success. It doesn't matter what it is that we succeed on - what's important is that we want success in everything we do, everything we prefer, want, fight for etc. But as you are well aware, wanting success and actualizing it are completely different things. Like everything in life, success does not just happen; there are prerequisites to success, which without them, you really cannot be sure that you will realize success.

So what is it that you need in life to become a success?

In order to succeed in life, you need a clear idea of where you are going and what it is you are going to do when you get there to remain there. It is one thing to succeed and another thing to maintain that success all your life. In life, I have come to learn one or two things about why some succeed in making something great out of their lives while the rest of the world either fails completely or keep running round in circles. For starters, I have come to realize that you cannot make anything worthwhile happen in your life when you do not have a direction. This is why I never fail to point out to people the need to find the purpose and discover what they are passionate about. If you do not have a cause for which you are willing to risk everything else, you cannot find a vision and a well defined mission that can be translated into millions and financial freedom.

Great ideas that change the way things are done in your niche or part of the world do not come to people who have no clearly defined purpose, vision and mission for their lives. One easy way to find strong mission that has the power to push you to success is to coin such purpose-driven missions from your passions.

Writing this book became important as it finally dawned on me that majority of people go through life without knowing what their lives are about and the steps they can take to live the kind of purpose-driven life that help them find a worthwhile mission they can translate into millions. In this book, we will be looking at the meaning of purpose, how to discover and define yours, how to generate world-changing ideas and steps you can take to turn such great ideas into millions. Let's begin.

Thanks again for downloading this book. I hope you enjoy it!

Mission to Millions:

How to find your Passion and Purpose in life

© **Copyright 2018 by Lucho - All rights reserved.**

This document is geared towards providing exact and reliable information in regards to the topic and issue covered. The publication is sold with the idea that the publisher is not required to render accounting, officially permitted, or otherwise, qualified services. If advice is necessary, legal or professional, a practiced individual in the profession should be ordered.

- From a Declaration of Principles which was accepted and approved equally by a Committee of the American Bar Association and a Committee of Publishers and Associations.

In no way is it legal to reproduce, duplicate, or transmit any part of this document in either electronic means or in printed format. Recording of this publication is strictly prohibited and any storage of this document is not allowed unless with written permission from the publisher. All rights reserved.

The information provided herein is stated to be truthful and consistent, in that any liability, in terms of inattention or otherwise, by any usage or abuse of any policies, processes, or directions contained within is the solitary and utter responsibility of the recipient reader. Under no circumstances will any legal responsibility or blame be held against the publisher for any reparation, damages, or monetary loss due to the information herein, either directly or indirectly.

Respective authors own all copyrights not held by the publisher.

The information herein is offered for informational purposes solely, and is universal as so. The presentation of the information is without contract or any type of guarantee assurance.

The trademarks that are used are without any consent, and the publication of the trademark is without permission or backing by the trademark owner. All trademarks and brands within this book are for clarifying purposes only and are the owned by the owners themselves, not affiliated with this document.

Table of Contents

Introduction

What Is Purpose And How Can You Discover Your Purpose For Living?

Discovering Your Purpose

Discovering Your Passions

    What Is Passion?

    Why Is Finding Your Passion Important?

    How Can You Find Your Passions?

Creating A Beautiful Business Idea From Your Mission

    Preparatory Steps To Make Your Business Idea Fly

Your Mission Is Your Dream: You Need A Strong Mission Statement

Turning Your Passion into Your Life Mission and the Mission into Millions

How Can You Turn Your Own Passion Into A Business?

Conclusion

Purpose

"Everyone has a purpose in life...a unique gift or special talent to give to others. And when we blend this unique talent with service to others, we experience the ecstasy and exultation of our own spirit, which is the ultimate goal of all goals."

-Deepak Chopra

Mission to Millions:

How to find your Passion and Purpose in life

What Is Purpose And How Can You Discover Your Purpose For Living?

Purpose can be defined as the reason why something is done, created, or exists. In line with your life, purpose can be said to be that very reason why you are gifted with the talents you were loaded with before being unleashed to your world. There is a reason why you are here. Your conception and birth were never made in error. Biology teaches us the struggle, which ensued the moment your parents mated with millions of sperm cells competing among themselves to get to the ovum of your mother to fertilize the egg. Among these millions of sperm cells, the sperm that became you was the only one strong and fast enough to outrun and outdo all others in that race/battle to succeed.

If you did not get pushed off the road during this life-forming race and battle and kept going until you got to where the main fertilization action took place, it is a clear indication that there is a reason for your being here. The onus now falls on you to discover your life's purpose, put your innate skills, talents and abilities into good use, make something great out of your life and make the world a better place for us all.

If all men discover purpose while here, the world would have become a paradise of sorts by now. Imagine a world where each person makes his/her own unique contribution and inventions. Imagine a world where everyone discovers purpose and leaves a positive impact. We wouldn't have been able to enjoy life as we do today if certain men and women in every generation do not say no to mediocrity, get committed to finding purpose, find purpose and leave the world better than they found it.

There is something you can do better than everyone else around you. There is always that unique gift you have and that talent you do not need anyone to teach you before you can pull things off in that particular area of life. You know where your passions lie, you know where your desires lie, you know the things you derive inexplicable joy from; such things should form the basis of your life's purpose. If it is motivating people you love doing and you discover you do it with a touch of uncommon excellence, the seeds for you to achieve your own mission to millions dream may be embedded in helping people get closer their goals and purpose in life.

We do have extremely successful motivational speakers like Tony Robbins, Nick Vujicic, Brian Tracy, Dr. Wayne Dyer, Zig Ziglar, Arnold Schwarzenegger, Jim Rohn and Les Brown who do many of the things that we all do yet have the unique gift to interpret the world and encourage others to reach for their dreams and hope for the best. Such motivational speakers discovered purpose, created a mission with which they have been able to bring in millions after millions of dollars doing what they love doing.

The secret to this is simple; one of the greatest secrets of success in life is to do what you love and love what you do, which is why I always advice that people find a way of connecting their missions to their passions. If your career is coined from what you have natural love for, you won't need to struggle to find the motivation to get started or stay put when things get tougher and require a greater level of mental toughness. Your innate talent could be in sports, literary world, entertainment, politics, leaderships, drawing, painting, acting, singing, playing a music instrument, etc. Whatever your talent and skills are, there lies in them the opportunities that can change the world and bring you those millions, the fame, people and all other trappings of success that have eluded you for long.

The important thing is to discover purpose. Paying attention to your skills is one great way to know in which direction your life should be taking and what your purpose for living could be all about.

Next, we will discuss how to discover your purpose.

Mission to Millions:
How to find your Passion and Purpose in life

Discovering Your Purpose

"The two most important days in your life are the day you were born and the day you discover the purpose why you were born".-Anonymous

One thing about purpose is that until you discover it, you will never feel fulfilled. This is because, no matter what you achieve in life, so long as it is not in line with the reason why you are here at this time, there will always be that empty feeling in your heart. Nothing can take the place of purpose in your life.

In fact, many go through life unsure what their life is about and how they can connect to purpose. You don't have to live like that. Take the steps outlined here now to discover purpose to enable you create those dreams and ideas that can put you on the path to turn your mission into millions.

- **You need more action in your life**

It is easier to work your way into finding the purpose for your life than thinking your way into it. In fact, no matter how good a thinker you are, it is almost impossible to find purpose by thinking and wishing. The best way to discover purpose is to take the NIKE advice and just do it. Yes, "Just Do It". That's the only way to discover purpose. Acting has a way of helping you get very clear ideas on life and your place in life.

Therefore, instead of spending all your life thinking whether your ideas will fly, whether you should try this or not, whether you will make money from your idea/business or not, whether you will enjoy that line of business or not, simply roll your sleeves, get to work and start taking necessary steps towards making your dreams come true by trying new things. Put those skills and talents into use. If oratory is your thing, maybe it is time to start gathering youths around you and teach them the principles of succeeding in life.

You don't have to be an expert to start, but you have to start before you can become an expert. By thinking over the options and possibilities without taking any actions to know what you can do and how well you can do them, you simply stand in your own way of discovering purpose and getting closer to turning your mission into millions. Get out of your own way now by taking the right steps and getting things done.

You may never discover purpose or know what your real passions are until you start doing what you have been thinking about all these years. I know a writer whose life ran round in circles for several years until he got the message of taking more action to discover purpose. He started writing short stories and sending them to publishing houses, and before he could write a couple of them, he had already received an acceptance letter from one of the publishing houses with a good publishing deal. Thus, a great writer was born, purpose was discovered, mission was created and millions were made through the sales of his books online and in bookstores around the world. Therefore, you must never forget that when it comes to discovering purpose to create the mission for your millions to come in, you need consistent action, with which comes the clarity you need to define purpose.

- **Work with your heart**

Most people fail to discover purpose because they depend on what their head says instead of relying on their hearts. You don't love with your head; you love with your heart. The heart is where the real love is. Whatever you love with your head won't stay for long because it has no strong roots. Emotions and passions are attributes of the heart. Your purpose is tied to your passions and you can only feel these passions and know what they are when you work more with your heart when trying to discover purpose. Those great ideas you need to change your life and the world at large won't come until you discover what it is your heart yearns for.

What are you passionate about? What are you in love with?

These should form the foundation of your purpose and it is never in the place of the head to know these things for sure. The head is logical and will try to give you reasons why such passions are unsafe, uncertain or probably not good enough. The heart loves and gets you into doing those things you love without judging or questioning.

You become more enthusiastic and motivated to explore those ideas and inspirations flooding into your heart when you are working with your heart. When you go with your head, you will find a million and one reasons to keep thinking and never take any actions. It is the head that tells you to wait until someone else tries and succeeds in that line of business you want to venture into before you launch yours; it is the head that tells you to wait until you have more experience, education or money before you start that business. Your head will always give you very logical and intelligent reasons not to keep exploring and when you listen to your head and follow it's dictates, you will never know what works and what doesn't, you will never know what you can do and what you can't handle, and when this becomes an accepted norm with you, discovering your purpose for living becomes next to impossible.

- **Drop the "ONE" idea**

It can be quite difficult to discover purpose and create your millions-unlocking mission when you are stuck with the idea that there is only one thing you can either do or you are meant to do. You will only be limiting your God-given potentials when you believe there is one thing you are meant to do and go out of your way to discover that one thing and nothing more. Your purpose must not be one thing you should be doing to make the world and your life better. You can be involved in so many things and still do them with purpose. Discovering purpose is all about discovering your passions and doing them in a way that helps you live a life of purpose.

I have seen sports people who venture into the production and marketing of sportswear, or become brand ambassadors for great sportswear manufacturing companies. They make more millions from endorsements than they make from participating actively in sports. I have seen teachers who take teaching to an entirely different level by creating an online teaching platform, creating teaching apps, becoming life coaches, writing great self-help books, and a whole lot of other things. You can be a fashion model and at the same time a designer. If the millions do not come from modeling, they will definitely come from your designer wears, shoes, handbags, perfume, etc. Remove the one thing idea when discovering and defining purpose. Most of the millionaire motivational speakers I mentioned earlier make their millions from some things that don't directly relate to speaking.

The main purpose of life is to live a life of purpose, and you cannot live a life of purpose without first discovering your passions and exploring them until you discover which one contains the secret code to your millions. Now that you understand how to find your purpose for being alive, the next thing we will discuss is how to find your passions because knowing your passion will open doors for discovering your purpose.

Passion

"Passion is energy. Feel the power that comes from focusing on what excites you."

-Oprah Winfrey

Mission to Millions:

How to find your Passion and Purpose in life

Discovering Your Passions

Most people have the problem of figuring out what their passions really are. How can you know where to go when you do not know where your passions lie? You can't discover purpose without discovering your passions. Well, it is really simple; the combination of your passions with daily actions helps you live a purposeful life.

Let me show you how you can get out of this rut. The problem is in your mental disposition and approach to discovering purpose. May be you have been asking yourself what your passions are instead of asking how you can solve other people's problems with your skills and talents or how you would love to help others live better, find purpose and fulfill destinies.

The easiest way to millions is to find a problem you can solve with your talents. Bill Gates came into his millions because he was able to solve a problem by making it easier for the non tech-savvy individual in the remotest parts of the world enjoy the computer through his Microsoft tools and inventions. Mark Zuckerberg came into his millions because of his ability to help people connect with anyone they wish to connect to in any part of the world and make online advertising more seamless. The motivational speakers who made millions came into their millions because they were able to come up with messages in books, videos and audios that help people overcome hopelessness, depression, anxiety, worry, fear, marital problems, stress, lack of visions, purposelessness, and several other things that keep them back.

What Is Passion?

It is simply that thing you are emotionally attached to. It is that thing you get crazy about and can work your ass off on because of the notion you have about that particular task. That thing you believe can rock your world is your passion. Your passion is worth finding and fighting for because it is the only feeling akin to the feeling you get when you fall in love with someone special. You wouldn't stop searching for love until you find it or let go when you finally find that special one for any reason in the world, would you? No, you wouldn't. That's the way you should treat your passions. Never rest until you find them and when you find them, never let them go.

But why do you need to find your passions? It is important you find your strong 'why' for finding your passion in order to be convinced it is really worth it.

Why Is Finding Your Passion Important?

There are so many ways finding and following your passions will help you succeed in life. Here are some benefits of finding your passions:

- Being passionate about something will persuade people to follow you.

- Your passion will persuade and motivate you to succeed more than any other thing

- They hold the seed for your financial success and that beautiful feeling of having lived a fulfilled and accomplished life.

How Can You Find Your Passions?

Finding your passion is as important as turning your passion into a million dollar business. But what steps can you take to help you discover what you are really passionate about and run with them?

Here are some steps you can take:

- **Start asking the right questions now**

Take a cursory look at your talents and ask how you can help people with what you know. How can you help? Don't say you don't know; there are many ways you can help. What you are passionate about is how you can help, and in it lies the seeds of your greatness.

- ✓ If you can help people fix their faulty computers, that's where your passion lies

- ✓ If you can help people learn to sing or play musical instruments, that's where your passion lies

- ✓ If you can help people build new apps and online marketing tools, that's where you passion lies

- ✓ If you can help people do anything or learn anything new, that's where your passion lies.

- ✓ If you can help people get a good laugh when they are down or depressed, that's where your passion lies

- ✓ If you can help bleeding marriages heal and get back to those early blissful grounds, that's where your passion lies

- **Ask yourself what you are good at and how you can help others**

Your answer is a pointer to where your passion lies. It is impossible to help others in areas where you have no passion. Once you find what it is you can do to help, you can start channeling your energy towards it until you can create a business around it.

It is easy to create your mission once you have discovered your passion and build your million dollar business around it. The passion itself is not the business. The problem you solve with your passion is the business for which people will be glad to pay you until your millions start trickling into your bank account.

If you have passion for helping others learn how to succeed, you can build a successful coaching business around that passion and make a great success out of it. Here is the best way to sum the connection between finding your passions, solving other people's problems and turning your mission into millions: *"Your million dollar opportunity resides at that point where your passions and skills intersected with other people's problems"*.

- **Create something new**

Whenever you succeed in creating something new, you are simply inventing something you can be passionate about. There are countless ways you can go about creating new things, which you can become passionate about and turn into a huge money-spinning business. Creating something new sets you apart from the crowd and sets you up for a mega success. What new things can you create as a way of finding a passion with money-making potentials? Let's see some possible examples here:

- Write superman or batman stories. If you are good with your pen, you could consider creating a series like Harry Porter. The writer of Harry Porter has made millions by turning out the scripts of that breathtaking series. You too can make money toeing same creative lines.

- Write a new book. There are different niches you could focus on depending on your specialty. You can write something on men's or women's health, how to stay young and healthy forever, you could write something on marriage/relationship such as how to make your marriage last forever, you could write a fiction and turn them into movies like the James Bond series, etc. One good book can be all you need to discover your passion is in writing good stories and also make your first million dollars.

- Create a new fashion trend. If you are a designer or just fashion-savvy, you could play with fashion ideas of the oldies and fuse them into some more current fashion ideas to create a new fashion sensation. You could be the new celebrity in designing and modeling circles and rake in some millions with your unique designs.

- Create a new app. We are in the digital age when apps seem to be the in thing. Everyone seems to need an app to get almost everything done. I think people are either becoming lazier by the day or the hustle and bustle of modern life leaves them with no choice than to rely on apps to do the simplest tasks like ordering their groceries, picking a taxi, organizing chores, etc. You could be that guy that brings the a new app to the different app stores.

One great thing about creating something new is the fact that it increases your odds of making that much sought after millions as there is always minimal competition in that area with very few daring to test the untested waters and chart new courses. One other amazing thing about creating new things is that you never can tell when you will create that new thing that will change the world and your entire life. A student named Mark began testing new waters and experimenting with building new sites somewhere in California Suburbs, even though he was nowhere among the coolest and most talented programmers at that time, at least he was daring enough to keep experimenting until he created the platform all of us enjoy today as Facebook. Yes, Facebook was an experiment, which turned out to be one successful experiment worth billions of dollars.

- **Start a new trend**

It becomes increasingly difficult to compete in any area once the idea ages. The older a trend or idea is, the harder it becomes to compete effectively and make something meaningful out of it. The truth is that thousands or probably millions of others got there before you thus lowering your chances of finding your passion there and succeeding with that passion. Passions follow success. Anything you succeed in, you become passionate about. It is impossible for you not to be passionate about something you are good at, makes you stand out, earns you money and accolades or increases your positive public perception and market value.

The good news here is there is always a new frontier opening up somewhere around you where the majority are either too unskilled to try anything or feel hopelessly incapable of competing in. Your little skills can make a whole lot of difference in such areas and establish you as a star to watch out for. Let's assume you started blogging and making money with Google AdSense as far back as the late 2000s when most internet users only went online to either check their emails or chat some friends on social media, and by the time they realized blogging was a goldmine, you had already gathered hundreds of thousands or even millions followers and had become established as a master in your niche. They won't be able to compete even if they decide to start blogging now. And with the level of success you have recorded, you would have become so passionate about blogging that it doesn't seem like work to you anymore. This same trend can be found in the rap world, among YouTubers, video game designers and app developers. The earliest entrants always lead the pack, discover passion and turn that passion into millions.

What can you do?

Look around you or your industry to discover budding and evolving opportunities early, become as skilled as you can be, put in your best and become passionate as you excel amidst minimal competition before others discover this trend and start hopping in.

- **Fuse several possibilities**

Relying on the education system might leave you grossly disappointed as the system is designed in such a way that your skills get narrowed as you climb higher on the academic ladder. Education will only help you discover your one best thing and push that option as far as possible.

However, most of us are not programmed to function exceptionally in any single area, but a combination of different options brings out the passionate side in most of us. Let's assume you are a gifted artist with a unique sense of humor. But the fact remains that an art degree won't hold lots of promises for you to break into the entertainment world and become the success you dream of becoming, and studying humor in college is way out of the question as there is no such college degree or subject. But you could be highly gifted with cartooning or painting or drawing.

Let's also assume you are an average business student with some decent sales skills and some basic programming abilities. You will be better suited to lead others who are better skilled in either of these two areas. The reason? A single skill hardly defines the most successful people - a fusion of skills does. You don't even have to be exceptionally skilled to turn your passions into a huge success, but you can become exceptional by making an exceptional combination of some of these skills you need to succeed with your mission and passions. You wouldn't consider Steve Jobs the best engineer, salesperson, programmer or businessman of his time. Nonetheless, he was gifted enough to know how to fuse all of his little skills in all of these areas to make something exceptional out of them and lead Apple to the global business arena. Therefore, your passion can come from a combination of different skills and abilities you need to become better at something you need to do well in order to succeed.

After finding what you are passionate about, you can now make a business out of it. Let's discuss how to make a powerful business idea from your mission next.

Passion and Purpose

"Allow your passion to become your purpose, and it will one day become your profession."

-Anonymous

Mission to Millions:
How to find your Passion and Purpose in life

Creating A Beautiful Business Idea From Your Mission

Knowing your purpose for living, your passions and defining your mission will not make a good business idea that can turn that mission into millions drop overnight.

You need to take some strategic steps towards turning that beautiful mission of yours into a business idea that will fly and bring you the financial success you have been dreaming of over the years. In coming up with a brilliant idea that will fly, there is need for you to ensure the idea is relevant in today's market by meeting a need in the life of your target customers.

Sometimes you do not need an entirely new idea before you can taste good success. Bill Gates only had to improve on what had already been invented by making the computer easily understandable and useful to the average non tech-savvy individual in the remotest part of the world. All you need might be to tweak an already existing product or service a little bit, add some new features to solve a pressing problem among users here and there in order to make it more appealing and useful to the end users.

To come up with the best ideas for your million dollar business, here are some techniques you could find handy:

- ✓ **Take another look at your talents and the skills you have developed**

In your line of work, you must have had several experiences and succeeded in a number of job roles more than everyone else at one time or the other. Think about all the companies and organizations you have either worked for or done business with. What were your roles on those jobs and how much did you enjoy doing what you did while with them? Which of those job roles came naturally to you and gave you utmost satisfaction even though you were not making as much money as you would have loved to make while on those jobs? Which of those jobs did you wish it never had to end due to the huge satisfaction you derived from it?

A good look at your historical work experiences will help you identify the connection between the jobs, business and projects you enjoyed the most with your purpose, passions, talents, mission and big dream. Establishing this important connection will help you see the area you should be looking at in terms of creating a business idea that will help you enjoy financial success sooner than later.

Also, make sure you rummage through your pastimes, hobbies, and all activities you wouldn't mind spending the rest of your life doing outside work such as caring for animals, the aged, the sick, developing apps that make home or office chores seamless, etc. By building a business based on something you naturally enjoy doing in some way, you can be sure to do what you love and love what you do for as long as you want to remain active. You never know where the unique business idea will drop from.

✓ Think about feasibility

Once you have written down everything you could remember about your job history and satisfaction, think about market trends and evolving business areas in your niche. There is always something new happening around for those who have eyes for picking up opportunities before they start appearing in the dailies. Here are some areas to pay more attention to:

- You can get instant inspiration and a unique business idea by looking at possible areas of growth in the financial sector, tech sector, and all other sectors.

- Study the businesses that are succeeding. There will always be those businesses that make profit even during the most severe recession and economic meltdown. Take a cursory look at how things work around such areas to see if there is a possible opportunity for you to cash in on the flow.

- Keep your eyes and ears open for market changes and opportunities they bring. Information is key. Take every necessary step to get the most updated information and market forecast from the experts. This will help you know where to invest and what to invest in. There are a number of online business magazines, which publish winding up petitions, details of liquidators, etc.

- Look out for products you can bring home to solve a pressing need around you. The internet has opened up countless opportunities for you to source products from any part of the world, bring them home and meet a pressing need.

- Think of the skills and abilities of people in your circle and see which of them you can team up with to float a great business in line with your mission.

- Keep an open mind for opportunities wherever you go. I once read a story about two friends who visited Calcutta - a poor Indian suburb where no one owned a pair of shoes-for possible business opportunities. One of the two friends looked around and said, *"These people are so poor that they cannot even afford a pair of shoes; there is* nothing for me here", and with that, he left. But his friend who had a more open mind for business opportunities said to himself, "*Everyone here needs at least a pair of shoes; this is a life-changing business opportunity for me*". And with that mindset, he went back to the U.S., contracted a shoe manufacturing company to produce affordable shoes for those Indians. He ended up selling several shiploads of shoes and thus came into wealth.

✓ **Don't forget the importance of thinking and looking forward**

If a business does not have any future growth potential, it makes no business sense coming up with such business idea and hoping it will help turn your mission to millions.

Always consider important local and global markets trends and demographics while choosing a business idea to run with. Follow media reports online and offline on new business trends, their feasibility and durability.

- ✓ **Envisage all the possibilities that come with being your own boss**

Finding the right business ideas that agree with your purpose, passions and mission may not be enough to spur you on and motivate you into taking action to make the beautiful idea become a functional business. You need motivation as you search for business inspiration and ideas. Here are some ways to find the motivation you need to get fired up for action:

- Think about all the rewards and benefits that come with running your own business such as taking better care of your health, spending more quality time with your loved ones, deciding what you earn and when you work, doing what makes you happy, having time for other pursuits such as academics and more certifications, etc

- Think about the emotional and financial gains of running that business. You want to go into that business in order to make more money. We all need the extra income to meet out monthly bill payments and afford those things we have always wanted to experience such as weekend gateways, holidays, new homes, cars, electronics, etc. A new business and the money it brings can make all these dreams come true. Think about these things and let them motivate you into taking action. Picture how beautiful your life will become with the increased income and let that beautiful picture keep you hungry for success until you have turned that mission into millions.

Preparatory Steps To Make Your Business Idea Fly

Make the dream a part of you. There is a reason why we advocate you pursue your passions and make sure you do what you love. For your beautiful dreams to become easily achievable, you must come to the point where life seems to have no real meaning without you living those dreams. Make sure this dream becomes an inseparable part of you. There are several ways you can make your dreams seem all-consuming. Here are a few ideas:

- **Write it down and paint it colorfully.** Paste it where it will be impossible for you not to see it first thing in the morning, as soon as you step into your office and last thing before bedtime. The more you look at the beautiful dream in written and pictorial representations, the more you get spurred to work on them until they become your daily living realities.

- **Meditate on them**. Meditation is the art of learning to focus on one thing at a time to gain mastery of it and enhance your concentration. You can begin by seating still and focusing on your breaths until you become accustomed to focusing on your breath and its rhythms. Once you master the art of focusing on your breath, you can take it a bit further by practicing visualization. This is where you picture the beautiful future achieving your beautiful dreams promises you. Do this as many times as possible during the day until you can't seem to think of anything else except achieving those dreams and living the life you pictured in those imaginary worlds of yours.

- **Think of everything you need to achieve this big dream and start** working towards acquiring them. The dream may seem bigger than you at first, but there are several things you can do in order to make the dream more feasible. What is it you dream of doing or becoming? Perhaps you wish to build a 100 million a year software company. What do you need to make this happen? Get the skills you need to build that 100 million a year software company, get the kind of investors who have the money or connection to make this dream fly; develop the marketing strategy to turn this mission into several millions of dollars, etc.

- **Believe this dream and don't stop believing it is possible**. If you stay positive and keep doing what you need to do, one day, your efforts will pay off and your dreams will come true. Stay with people who make you believe it is possible and stay away from people and habits that make you doubt your ability to pull it off.

- **Share this dream**. In case you are still bent on going solo and went through the whole process of coming up with the million dollar idea and crafting your winning mission statement without getting anyone else involved, you may have to reconsider at some point. I have seen people carry their big dreams in their head around without sharing it with anyone who might help make it come true and end up carrying them to the grave because they either lacked the technicality or the financial wherewithal to make those dreams happen. You can find someone you can trust with your business idea and share with them. Your parents can invest in your business idea. Your siblings can invest in your business idea. Your boss can invest in that idea. Your religious leader might be interested. Just make sure you do not give every detail way when sharing such ideas to avoid losing out entirely.

- **Plan and never stop planning.** You will end up getting whatever you plan for in life one way or the other. Find time to sit with your dream and plan out your strategies and steps to success. Learn what you need to learn, study what you need to study, and practice when you should until you are well equipped and ready to act. Break down your dreams into small goals and sub-tasks, time each sub-task and allocate time to each task.

Once you are done with planning, write your mission statement and take action to turn the mission into millions. Let's discuss mission statement in the next chapter.

Your Mission Is Your Dream: You Need A Strong Mission Statement

You need a big picture. Something you can always look at and feel motivated. What passions have you discovered? What is the purpose for your life? How can you help others with your talent? I'm sure you know the answers to these questions by now.

The next question you should ask yourself is: How can you turn your passion into your life mission? What is a mission? Your mission is your life's major desire and intent. In other words, your mission is your life's dream. It is what your life is about. It is purpose. It is what you hope to achieve at the end of the day. It is what you wish to see your life become. It is what you hope to help your customers achieve with your products and services. And the best way to capture it is with a well crafted mission statement.

How can you create a powerful mission statement that can inspire, motivate, and initiate the right actions and responses? Let's explore further:

- ✓ ***Writing a strong mission statement***

Your mission can be captured in a statement known as your mission statement. Your mission statement is a reflection of your purpose and your vision.

It is important you come up with a statement that will encompass every aspect of your business. Before you can go about carving out your mission statement, there are some important questions you need to put into consideration. A powerful mission statement can be the driving force you need to wake up each day and work on your dreams with utmost focus until you achieve them. Here are some important questions to consider while carving your mission statement:

- What is your reason for going into this line of business and what do you hope to achieve at the end of the day? The answer to this question should contain a hint of your long term goal. What do you wish to achieve for yourself? What do you wish to achieve for your family? What do you wish to help your customers achieve? Think about that passion that ignited your desire to start up the business and what can keep that passion aglow.

- Who and where are your target markets? In what ways can what you wish to offer affect the lives of your loved ones as well as your customers? How can it contribute to their success now and in the future? How can it make their lives better?

- What image do you wish to convey to your audience about

your business? Everyone will have his or her different perceptions about you and your business. The picture you create about your business will help shape their perception about you and what you offer.

- What makes your product and services better than everyone else? Don't just make claims without justifications.

- How does what you offer differ from the products and services offered by your competitors? What can you do better, faster and at a cheaper rate? How do you plan to use the weaknesses of your competitor to your own advantage?

- How do you wish to harness existing marketing tools and technologies to reach your business goals? A good description of your intended strategies will help you focus your energies on your major goals.

- What is your business philosophy? Writing down the business philosophies you subscribe to gives you clear answers to these questions and helps you understand why you are sticking to the mission you have chosen.

✓ **Crafting the best mission statement**

Anything with a lasting value will require thoughtful planning, time and efforts. Whether you are pursuing a professional career or floating new business, crafting a strong mission statement will help you solidify your reason for getting involved in that profession and clarify the motivating factors driving you to do what you plan to do. These tips will help you make your mission statement as powerful and stimulating as any mission statement can ever be:

- **Involve someone or others who have one or two ideas about what you want to venture into.** You don't have to be scared of involving someone else - most business fly when there are healthy collaborations. When it comes to crafting your mission statement, getting one or two more ideas will help you get things right. If you do not have any investors or partners whose opinions you can rely on, you can consider seeking the opinion of your spouse, a family member or friend with a sound mind. Hiring the services of a consultant may not be out of place too. These people can help you spot strengths, weaknesses and pitfalls you might have missed. However, you must ensure you only involve supportive people who wish to see you succeed.

- **Set adequate time aside to craft your mission statement.** Your mission statement may not be more than one sentence. However, some mission statements can take up a whole page but not more. Whether it is one sentence mission statement or one page, you need time to think things over, answer the relevant questions, consult whoever you need to consult, do some experimentation and sampling before arriving at the most ideal statement for your mission and purpose. Remember this statement is meant to serve as a beacon of inspiration to you and every other person involved in your business. So make it as powerful as possible.

- **Adequate preparation is key.** Plan a date and inform everyone involved in the business. Get all relevant materials such as writing materials ready. You may start by intimating the others who may not really understand the importance of a mission statement, what it is all about and how powerful it can be. Go with a list of topics to think and talk about as well.

- **You need a lot of brainstorming.** Every idea should be considered and weighed no matter how silly it sounds. Discuss or think about the questions listed previously. Look at sample mission statements. If you are working with a group, you can record everyone's answers to those questions, then, ask each one of them to write a mission statement for the business. Read the different statements out loud. Criticize them, select the most suitable bits and fix the pieces together to get the most apt mission statement for your business.

- **Don't forget the power of using catchy words and phrases.** Experts opine that when it comes to mission statements, every word counts. So once you have a basic idea of what your mission statement should look like, polish them to create dynamic images in the mind of everyone concerned with the aim of initiating action. You can employ upbeat verbs and adjectives to spice things up a bit.

Once you are done crafting your mission statement, make sure you place it where everyone will see it. Paste it on the wall of your office, paste it on the company vehicle, write it at the back of your business cards, flyers, and all other promotional materials. Make sure it appears on all pages in your company website also. Once you are done with this, let the action begin and watch the money roll in.

Let's take this discussion further where we will discuss how to turn your passion into your mission statement and the mission into millions.

Turning Your Passion into Your Life Mission and the Mission into Millions

Turning your mission into millions begins with turning your passions into a lucrative business. No matter what you are passionate about, you can turn it into a booming business. Most of the people whose praises you sing today in the sporting, entertainment and business world are people who discovered their passions and turned them into businesses that had the ability to turn their life missions into millions.

Are you passionate about football or any other sporting activity? You can turn that passion into a money spinning career. Every international footballer you know today started playing football at a street corner in some part of the world. The most successful footballers are not necessarily the most talented. The only difference is that while some were comfortable with having that sports they are passionate about as a hobby, the ambitious ones worked hard to improve their skills and thus turned those passions into very lucrative careers. You know how much some of the biggest English premiership clubs splash on these star footballers every season in the transfer market. These are talented footballers who have succeeded in turning their passions into millions.

If it is singing, writing, acting, comedy or public speaking you are passionate about, that passion has in it the seeds of your greatness and millions. I know so many authors who make millions every year from the sales of their books around the world. I know singers who will never stop making millions even after they die. I know actors who will never be broke a day in their lives for as long as they live. These people are not the most gifted singers, comedians, actors, public speakers or instrumentalists. They are only exceptional because they turned their passions into lucrative careers. The most talented singers are littered all around the streets and suburbs of the word. You can find them as lead singers in church bands; you can find some of the most gifted comedians in local comedy troupes in some of the remote villages of the world. The ones who make it to the big screen are not necessarily the most talented - they only learnt to apply the principles you are about to learn in this section.

The best app developers may never go beyond building a couple of cool apps or websites for their businesses and some for friends. Imagine if Mark Zuckerberg had been satisfied with creating cool websites for fun. If he had not kept experimenting to see how he could turn his passion for developing and coding into a lucrative business, the world wouldn't have had the seamless business and networking platform we know as Facebook today.

You may be passionate about e-commerce and online business, and there are several million dollar opportunities in that field as well. Jack Ma, who is believed to be the richest man in China today, turned his passion for running e-commerce site into an international business that has given him billions of dollars. Today, most importers and exporters rely on Alibaba.com for sourcing products and buyers from different parts of the world, thus making the import-export business easier and safer than anyone would have ever thought possible.

How Can You Turn Your Own Passion Into A Business?

Let's see some steps you can take to achieve this:

❖ **Find a void and fill it.** What problems can you solve with the skills borne out of your passions? This is one important question you must ask yourself before finding a void you can fill with that which you love doing. Let's assume you love singing or cracking jokes to make people happy. There is a career opportunity in that passion as many people are looking for ways to escape depression, worry and anxiety. If you become a standup comedian or a singer, these people will be willing to pay in order to watch or listen to your perform. In business arenas, look for a problem you can create a solution to. If you are passionate about makeups, you could create products that help women look younger and more beautiful without any risk of developing skin reactions, blemishes and wrinkles over time. Most of the makeup products and kits in the market come loaded with chemicals that leave the skin looking worse than it used to be before the individual started applying the makeups. You can replace such harmful or toxic ingredients with something less irritating to the skin.

❖ **Practice until you are the master in that art.** Being passionate about something is never enough to bring your skills on that art to the point where you can gain enough mastery of it to turn it into a lucrative career. Everyone who has ever been named world best footballer is known to train more than everyone else. If it is singing you are passionate about, you need to practice until you have developed that skill to the point where people will be willing to part with their hard earned cash just to listen to you sing. You may have to experiment with different business models and keep practicing until you are able to tell what works and what doesn't. And with that knowledge, you can push your business along the line that produces the best results. If yours is to build sites or apps, keep building them until you can come up with the very best. If yours is writing, keep writing until your editor can go through the entire manuscript without finding a single odd sentence structure.

- ❖ **Know how much value people place on your skills by offering your services for a fee.** You need to test the waters before you launch the business or career fully. Sample opinions by asking those whose opinions you can always count on how much they will be willing to pay to watch you perform, play or sing. How much they will be willing to pay to have you design their next business app or website. Such samplings will help you know how valuable you and what you offer hold in the market in terms of monetary values.

- **Don't neglect the power of good networking.** Most times, talents and skills are not just enough to put you out there for the world to see what you have got and pay for your uncommon skills. Nothing is more common than failures with great talents. I have seen great talents languish in penury and misery, and I have also seen people with not-so-great talents to world charts in sports, tech, entertainment, politics, etc. What set the latter apart from the former? Lack of opportunities. Your network brings you closer to opportunities where your talent, passion and mission can bring in the millions. You will need a manager, agent, partners or mentors depending on what field you are venturing into.

Mission to Millions:

How to find your Passion and Purpose in life

Conclusion

We have come to the end of the book. Thank you for reading and congratulations for reading until the end.

No talent is good enough to turn into money on its own without the right efforts and actions. First, you need to sharpen those inborn talents to the point where you gain enough mastery to turn it into a career. Create financial dreams and missions from those passions, find opportunities and problems you can solve with your passion, and watch your bank account bulge every other day. I hope the book has taught you how you can transform your life by leveraging on your passion, purpose and mission to make millions.

If you found the book valuable, can you recommend it to others? One way to do that is to post a review on Amazon.

Mission to Millions:

How to find your Passion and Purpose in life

We would greatly appreciate it if you could leave a review for this book on Amazon!

Thank you and good luck!

About the Author

Lucho is a life coach and author of self-help titles. His self-help titles include the Law of Attraction book series- **Becoming a Money Magnet, Finding Love, Attracting Happiness; Success Cycle : the 3 Simple secrets to an unending success** and **Mission to Millions : How to find your passion and purpose in life (Making money with your passion)** and each one concentrates on distinct aspects of what it takes to become happy, successful or content.

In his free time, Lucho enjoys playing badminton, traveling, writing, walking, playing with his dogs and practicing yoga. He loves reading self-help books and devotes part of his time to volunteering in a soup kitchen, where he helps to prepare food for those who are less fortunate.

In the future, he plans to write more and continue with his charitable works.